# à la Cart

## THE SECRET LIVES OF GROCERY SHOPPERS

# HILLARY CARLIP

# à la Cart

## THE SECRET LIVES OF GROCERY SHOPPERS

### Photographs by Barbara Green

Virgin Books USA    New York

All photographs by Barbara Green

All make-up and hair by Dominie Till except for Graciela, Estelle, Troy, Bernadette, and Lloyd by Chris Nelson. Make-up and hair for both author photos by Hilda Levierge.

Distributed by Macmillan

FIRST EDITION

Designed by Laura Lindgren

Library of Congress Cataloging-in-Publication Data
Carlip, Hillary.
  A la cart : the secret lives of grocery shoppers / Hillary Carlip. — 1st ed.
     p.  cm.
  ISBN-13: 978-1-905264-17-9
  ISBN-10: 1-905264-17-8
  1.  American wit and humor.  I. Title.
  PN6165.C363 2008
  818'.54—dc22                     2007042555

Printed in China

10 9 8 7 6 5 4 3 2 1

# The photos you are about to see are all me...

Don't worry—they're not my vacation snapshots, or cheesy pics of me posing with my dogs wearing hats. The photos are of me as twenty-six different people—of varying ages, genders, ethnicities, and sexual orientations. They're people whose lives I've imagined and embodied after stumbling upon one of the most intimate and revealing documents they've left behind—*their shopping lists.*

I was a teenager when I found my first discarded shopping list in a cart at the Safeway market in Westwood, California. Among the items jotted on a pre-printed form were: *"Sara Lee German Chocolate Cake, Pepperidge Farm Coconut Cake, Van de Kamp's Orange Rolls, Van de Kamp's Windmill Cookies."* I immediately pictured "Betty"—she played bridge, went to the beauty parlor weekly, had a secret smoking habit, and, having never taken a chance in her life, felt closer to Mr. Van de Kamp than to her own husband.

From then on I've been obsessed with collecting these snapshot scraps of human nature. Every time I discover an abandoned shopping list—in the produce aisle at Albertsons, on the street in front of a Korean market, or in grocery store parking lots across America—I feel as if I'm getting a glimpse into a stranger's life.

From the items included, the style of handwriting, the paper and pen/pencil/computer used, and even misspellings ("*Aunt Spray*"), I can't help but imagine the women and men who left behind their lists.

Having spent much of my life in disguises—as a child who thought becoming other elaborate personas would be far more interesting than being myself, and in my later years as a performance artist—the next step seemed only natural. Why not *become* the imagined authors of these found lists? I did this not just by dressing up, but by going through a transformation physically and emotionally. I delved deeply into their psyches: first, being photographed as the shoppers in various grocery stores, then writing short narratives about each of them.

Photographer and co-conspirator Barbara Green, who can take a close-up shot of the speckled floor tiles in a market and create a masterpiece, befriended these twenty-six shoppers along with me.

I loved hanging out with Pammy, the ex-porn sensation, as everyone ogled me being her, one man offering to carry my groceries to my car even though he didn't work at the market. And as creepy as it was to become Derrick, the tortured Goth boy and author of one of the most haunting lists: *"Mouse Traps, Cheese, Mouse,"* I had compassion for him, having felt like an outsider many times myself.

I want to eat pepperoni and pineapple pizza with Deb, work on Graciela's float for the Gay Pride parade, kick back and watch *Pants-Off Dance-Off* with Woody, and applaud Tootles as she breaks wind at her stand-up gig at the Institute for Phobic Awareness.

On countless occasions I've been tempted to snatch lists right out of shoppers' hands—especially the woman at Whole Foods who was buying soy milk as she was breast-feeding her baby. But then it would lack the mystery, the pleasure of getting to know these strangers, sight unseen, through their abandoned lists.

I hope you enjoy getting to know them as much as I have.

XO Hillary Carlip

# Graciela

Graciela never dreamed that La Casa Verde Pequeña, the restaurant her parents left to her and her two brothers, would go from barely getting by in a run-down neighborhood to becoming one of the trendiest restaurants in San Antonio, booked weeks in advance.

¡Viva la gentrification and the gays! She loves her clientele—the muscle boys, the drag queens, and the trannies who all call her "Mami," even though she has six kids and eleven grandchildren of her own.

When she was fourteen, Graciela and her brothers came to the United States to reunite with their parents, who had immigrated from Guadalajara five

Cafe 2
Azucar
Leche
Zanaorias
PanPers
Juga mansana
Margarina
Pan
Wipers
Jamon
Pepas
Servietas

Chanpu
Apio
Zuchini
Calabas
Pepinos
quezo du
Brocoli
esperagas
Mansana
Granbery
Naranjas

years before in search of a better life. They had a tiny taco stand and Graciela went right to work there, never finishing high school. Though she may not know the three Rs, especially in English, she learned a lot about business as she watched her parents expand their restaurant over the years. It's just as well they're not around today to see what's become of La Casa Verde Pequeña—very traditional people, her parents wouldn't understand that Wednesday nights are Miss Latina Drag contests!

Lately, Graciela's been exhausted. Between managing the restaurant, taking care of her homebound husband who has a chronic kidney condition, helping her son and daughter-in-law who live with her with their new baby (he's so colicky, he cries all night! Mira!), shopping for her granddaughter's Quinceañera, and cooking her famous ham and vegetable casserole for the event, it's surprising Graciela has any energy left to plan La Casa Verde Pequeña's float for the upcoming Gay Pride parade.

Although the regulars keep insisting that Mami needs to be front and center on the float, the base of which is a giant tostada shell, Graciela feels she might scare away business looking as run-down as she does.

Time for a makeover! And she knows just the drag queens who can help.

# Heather

**I**n high school, Heather tried to kill herself twice. Growing up in a small town in Wisconsin where most people read Danielle Steele and Stephen King and didn't even know who Baudelaire, Proust, or Kerouac were, all Heather wanted to do during her miserable adolescence was leave—any way she could.

In her freshman year of college she was dumped by her Medieval Literature professor, whom she was sleeping with, and that was it. She bought a cheap one-way ticket to Paris and split.

With only a backpack, three books, and a hundred bucks, she roamed the streets of the City of Light, more than once contemplating throwing

*INFUSIUM 23*
*glue.—Eyelash*
*clipper*
*Hair spray*

14

herself into the Seine. At least there her death would be literary and romantic.

But one blustery winter day, Heather wandered into the Church of Sainte-Madeleine and found a slice of sun streaming through stained-glass windows, illuminating a statue of Joan of Arc. She stared at the sculpture for hours, soaking in Joan's courage. Here was someone who had vision, a clear purpose. Someone who fought to the end for what she believed. Would Heather ever believe in anything that strongly?

As if Joan's spirit had entered her and was guiding her toward some destined path she might not have wandered on herself, the very next day Heather met Mélanie, a kindred spirit with more tattoos than Heather, who had not only read Baudelaire, Proust, and Kerouac, but could recite entire passages from their books as well. Mélanie turned Heather on to the Suicide Girls, a popular Web site featuring alternative, sex-positive, indie-style, punky pin-up girls. Heather sent in an application, was chosen, and has been posing for edgy, sexy photos ever since. And despite its name, to Heather, being a Suicide Girl has much more to do with life than anything she has felt before.

Though her calling may not be as noble as Joan's mission to save France from English domination, for the first time ever, Heather feels like she is following a vision. And, finally, she doesn't want to go down in flames anymore.

# Woody

When Woody decided it was time to settle down, he thought he would expand his dating pool and sign up on eHarmony. Although it took him three weeks to fill out his personal profile, he did come up with some "really good stuff."

**ABOUT ME:**

I'm a Lady's Man and that is true until now. Today I am ready to meet just one Special Lady with NO KIDS and try to make something work. I'm hard working and have NO BANKRUPTCIES.

**LIFESTYLE:**

I am looking for: A special Lady who don't have kids. Would you relocate?: Yeah, especially if her place has cable. And a nicer shower would be good too.

Relationship status: Looking.

Children: 4 Nieces and 3 Nephews.

Plan on having children: Because of a work accident I can't have no kids.

Activity level: Very Active. Sometimes sweating but not too much.

Zodiac sign: The Bull. But I'm not really like that.


PHYSICAL INFO:

I am: 5'7"

I weigh: 170 pounds

My hair is: Brown and long.

Facial hair?: Got a Fu Manchu.

My eyes are: Brown almost Black. And sexy.

My body style is closest to: The guy who sings lead in Aerosmith but his lips are bigger.

**CAREER AND MISC INFO:**

My education: I got a GED so that makes me a high school graduete.

Occupation: Construction.

Annual income: Will tell you later if we like each other.

After work I like to: Kick back with a beer and watch cable.
Especially like watching *Pants-Off Dance-Off*.

Political orientation: Straight.

**I AM LOOKING FOR:** Single special Lady with NO KIDS. Curvy, she should have a job and NO BANKRUPTCIES.

"That's it! A newt!" June felt like private investigator Kinsey Millhone, from Sue Grafton's mysteries, when she finally solved her son Jonah's birthday party dilemma.

The youngest of three boys, almost eight-year-old Jonah was recently diagnosed with Tourette's Syndrome. June and her husband, Jules, were devastated, but relieved when the doctor explained it wasn't the kind of Tourette's where one uncontrollably shouts out profanities. Instead, Jonah has

1  radio shack
2  volley ball
3  p o p
4  ice cream
5  paper plates, cups, plastic ware
6  fudge sauce
7  cake mix
8  icing
9  basket ball
10  aquarium, clean it
11  light bulb for aquarium
12  n e w t
13  book on newt
14  rock, tree branch
15  filter materials
16  gravel
17  basket ball
18  shirt for jules

constant throat clearing, facial tics with eye blinking, and an obsession with counting things. He has to make sure everything is in thirteens: He must take thirteen steps at a time, have thirteen shirts in his closet, chew each bite of food thirteen times, and brush his teeth with thirteen strokes.

Everything was smooth sailing with the plans for Jonah's birthday party—which included cake, ice cream, and presents at the Flying Wheels Roller Skating Rink—until the day before, when Owen Mills got head lice and Mrs. Mills said her son wouldn't be able to attend. That cut the guest list to *twelve*. June invited anyone and everyone she could think of, including their gardener, but found no one who could come to the party.

That's when she thought of THE NEWT. She would get it as one of Jonah's gifts, bring it to the Roller Rink, and convince her son that, as his new pet, the newt counted as guest number thirteen.

Some days June thinks that maybe the swearing kind of Tourette's would be easier to deal with.

# Maggie

*E*ver since she was nine years old and a babysitter snuck her into the R-rated movie *Pretty Woman,* Maggie knew what she wanted to be when she grew up—a hooker with a heart of gold.

She figured out quickly that this was not something to tell her teachers and parents' friends when they asked about her dreams for the future. So she'd always answer, "I want to be a nurse." After all, they were pretty much the same thing—taking care of someone's needs—though with streetwalking you could make a lot more money, and have a much better chance of meeting a rich businessman who would sweep you off your fire escape.

So just like Julia Roberts' character, Vivian, Maggie dropped out of high

Tampax
Baby Shampoo
Notebook
Gum
Vaseline Intensive Care Lotion
Aunt Spray
Doritos
Thongs

school in the eleventh grade and left her small town for the streets of Hollywood. Oh, she knew it would be tough; she remembered the low-lifes Vivian hung around before her lucky break. But she followed Vivian's every step—from finding a roommate who gave her valuable vocational advice, to staking out the same turf between Bob Hope's and Ella Fitzgerald's stars on Hollywood Boulevard. And just like in the film, she and her roommate vowed to never have a pimp—"We say who, we say when, we say how much!"

Maggie now knows that they left a few things out of the movie—like black eyes, getting busted, and crystal meth. She's been in the business for ten years, and still hasn't found her prince. But a few months ago she signed up as a call girl with an escort service (she didn't go back on her vow since she's not really working for a pimp, but a high-class madam), and her clientele has greatly improved.

Watching *Oprah* recently, Maggie listened to a panel of experts say that if you visualize something you desire strongly enough, you can attract it to you and make it happen. So she's been wandering around Beverly Hills, imagining herself in the *Pretty Woman* Rodeo Drive shopping spree montage—buying Gucci originals and Louis Vuitton bags, then slapping down her client/prince-to-be's Platinum Card, showing the salesgirls who give her attitude that they're messing with the wrong lady.

Tonight Maggie had a "date" booked with a fancy lawyer she was excited to meet, but she had to cancel it last minute because she got her period.

"Shit," she wailed while settling onto her bed with a heating pad, "I bet this never happened to Julia Roberts!"

# Estelle ("Tootles")

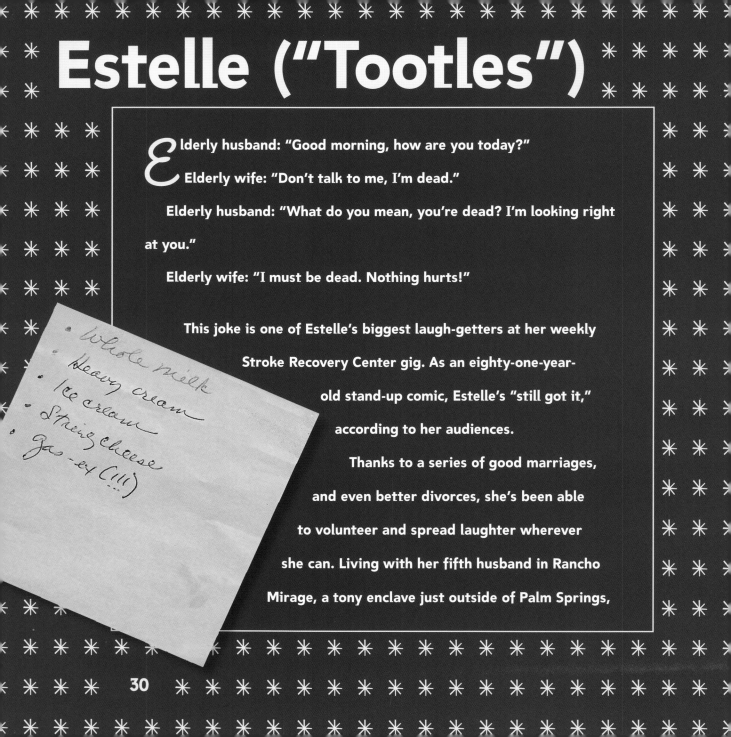

**E**lderly husband: "Good morning, how are you today?"

**Elderly wife:** "Don't talk to me, I'm dead."

**Elderly husband: "What do you mean, you're dead? I'm looking right at you."**

**Elderly wife: "I must be dead. Nothing hurts!"**

This joke is one of Estelle's biggest laugh-getters at her weekly Stroke Recovery Center gig. As an eighty-one-year-old stand-up comic, Estelle's "still got it," according to her audiences.

Thanks to a series of good marriages, and even better divorces, she's been able to volunteer and spread laughter wherever she can. Living with her fifth husband in Rancho Mirage, a tony enclave just outside of Palm Springs,

Estelle performs for such organizations as Desert AIDS Project, the Palm Springs Women's Club, the Institute for Phobic Awareness, and RSVP, Retired Senior Volunteer Program, though personally she's not planning on retiring till she hits 100!

One day she was entertaining abused kids in the Self Esteem program at the Barbara Sinatra Children's Center, and when exiting the stage, called out her signature sign-off, "Toodles!" Only she was experiencing some flatulence issues, and accidentally let a big one rip. The kids had never laughed so hard in their lives, and the staff could barely contain themselves as well. A consummate professional, Estelle made it seem like she farted on purpose and called up another one, declaring, "What I meant to say was "TOOT-les!" She received the longest standing ovation of her sixty-year career.

Now in the greater Palm Springs area, everyone knows Estelle as

"Tootles." And every time she performs, kids and seniors alike wait for her big finish.

So as lactose intolerant as she may be, Estelle eats as much dairy as she wants, and uses Gas-X only when she's not booked for a gig. After all, she can't let her fans down!

# Tuyen

T uyen remembers a lot of things about her childhood in Vietnam. Like Tết Trung Thu, the Mid-Autumn Festival where children parade on the streets carrying colorful lanterns, and receive moon cakes filled with lotus seeds, sweet bean paste, and a bright egg yolk in the center to represent the moon. She also remembers much sorrow and the ravages of war, and how she was always comforted by being in the kitchen, watching her mother cook.

Fleeing to the United States when Tuyen was five, her parents vowed to keep a traditional household and imbue their children with Vietnamese culture. They made Tuyen and her brother, Quan, speak only Vietnamese at home

- hành lá
- cần tây
- hành củ
- Salad
- trứng
- ớt
- Giá
- ngò có tốt thi
- mua
- Orange Juice.
- Yogurt (fruit bottom)

34

by pretending they didn't understand what the kids were saying when they spoke English. But if Tuyen and Quan spoke Vietnamese to each other in school, classmates teased them, calling them "F.O.B.s," for "Fresh Off the Boat."

When Tuyen was sick, her mother would "Beat the Wind" out of her, dipping a fifty-cent piece in Vicks VapoRub, then vigorously running the edge of the coin up and down Tuyen's back so illness ("the poisonous winds in the body") would fly away. One day at school, Tuyen's teacher noticed the red slashes all over her back and called in social services. It took a lot of explaining to get them to understand.

So when her parents recently came to dinner to meet her new boyfriend, Kevin, Tuyen wanted to soften the blow she knew they would inevitably feel since Kevin is a NASCAR-loving ex-Marine from Texas. She made one of her mother's favorite traditional dishes, Bánh xèo

—Vietnamese sizzling crêpes—and even shopped (several times) for the ingredients at the 99 Ranch market in Little Saigon.

Tuyen wasn't at all prepared when, in the excitement of the evening, Kevin got down on his knee and proposed to her! Her mother politely excused herself from the table, saying she felt ill. Tuyen knew that it wasn't the fish sauce, but that her mother was sickened by realizing that the family tree would eventually fade to white.

As Kevin and her father finished dinner, Tuyen went into the bedroom and offered her mother some help. She dug up a fifty-cent piece, some Vicks VapoRub, and started to "Beat the Wind" out of her.

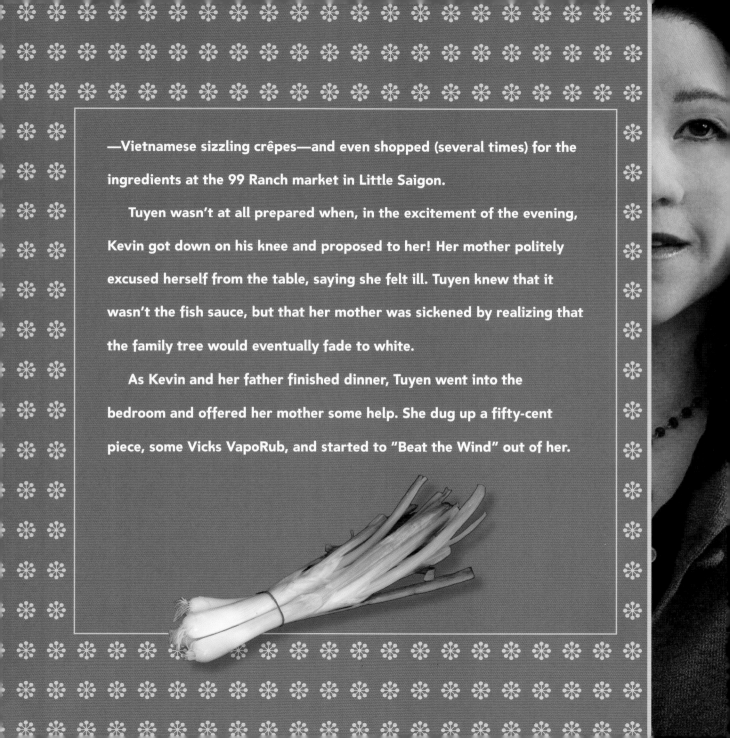

# Deb

"It's just not fair," Deb often cries to Bruno, her boyfriend of two years. "You can eat whatever you want and your body fat is three percent. I eat one Triscuit and I blow up like Star Jones before her procedure!"

Deb resents Bruno for more than the fact that he can freely carbo-load. He's always telling her how fat she is and watching over everything she eats. "Who are you?" she snapped recently, "freakin' Jenny Craig?!" On top of it all, Bruno's been making Deb train extra hard with him to compete in the International Aerobic Championships. Last year he got to the men's semi-finals (losing to a guy he swears was on 'roids), but this year he wants to up his chances of winning by competing in more

**SHOPPING LIST**

Power bars
protein powder
Splenda
Soy Milk
Chips Ahoy

categories—including Mixed Pairs. *Or so he says.* Deb thinks it's just an underhanded ploy to get her on a tougher training regime. What's next, is he gonna make her get lipo, a tummy tuck, and a boob job?

After teaching aerobics and step classes all day, the only thing Deb wants to do is go home, sit on the couch, and order a large pepperoni and pineapple pizza from Domino's. But Bruno has put her on a strict diet (she might as well be wearing one of those electronic ankle bracelets!) and makes her rehearse their routine for hours after work.

Deb loves Bruno. And she can't deny that she digs having a hot boyfriend with a six-pack to die for. It used to make her feel attractive. But now she just feels crappy about herself all the time, and is terrified that she'll go into a tailspin and start binging and barfing again. Bulimic through high school, Deb spent two months at the Renfrew Center, an eating disorder treatment facility in Philadelphia, after going down to eighty-five pounds. Although she's maintained a healthy weight ever since, she's never told Bruno about her past, and has vowed she never will. He just wouldn't understand. Besides, she sees how it is for him at the gym. He could hook up with hundreds of more attractive, thinner girls who would all want to be his Mixed Pairs partner—in more ways than one.

So what should she do?

She'll figure it out over some Chips Ahoy.

# Sally

E leven-year-old Sally once heard her father say she was an "accident," although she's not sure what that means. Born ten years after her brothers and sister, all she knows is that they get everything they want—her parents just gave Claire a new iPod, Danny went on a white-water rafting trip, and Brian got a flat-screen plasma TV for his room—and all Sally gets are dumb, girly things she hates, like a sewing machine and a Jazz Diva Barbie doll. Brian is supposed to share his computer with her but he always shoos her off, and once, when she finally got on, she found some naked pictures of his girlfriend. Ewww. The only cool thing that she ever got was from her Aunt Carol, who knows Sally loves the TV special

Sally—
Bring home
all my change!

eggs
milk
mini pimentos
celery
Cocoa Puffs
napkins
paper plates
sweet pickles
dill " ..
paprika

*It's the Great Pumpkin, Charlie Brown*, and gave her a vintage Snoopy sweatshirt.

Sally's mother and father both work so they're never around. Neither are her brothers and sister, who are young enough to still live at home, but old enough to get away with not doing anything. But if Sally doesn't do all her chores (including shopping for her mother!) she gets no allowance or is even grounded. It's sOOoooO not fair!

At least she has her friend Matt to hang out with. They ride bikes and go up and down the elevator in the twenty-three-story office building down the street. Mostly they play Sims 2, since, unlike Sally's parents, Matt's mom and dad give him cool things like his own computer and games. Sally spends hours on Sims 2 in the virtual world she's created—with a killer home in Pleasantview, ten TVs, five computers, an Olympic-size swimming pool, a drum set, and a bowling alley. She

"lives" there with two stay-at-home parents (and makes *them* do all the chores!) and one baby sister she can boss around. She gets anything she wants, and can even order Chinese food, day or night.

If Sally's parents in real life treat her like an "accident," then why should she ever listen to them? When she grocery shops for her mom, she's gonna spend all her change! And if she gets in trouble, so what? She'll just run away and go home to Pleasantview.

# Darcy

**B**efore she learned her ABCs, Darcy was taught that CAPITALISM SUCKS and ANARCHY RULES!! She spent her childhood in a van, going cross country to gigs with her parents who were in a punk band and played on the same bill with The Circle Jerks, The Dead Kennedys, and Black Flag. Darcy's dad teased that she wasn't home-schooled, she was "van-schooled!" Early on, Darcy discovered she was a pretty good artist and illustrator, and drew all the fliers for the band's gigs. When she was fourteen and her parents split up, Darcy was given the choice of staying on the road with her dad or going to live with her mom in an Airstream on an Indian reservation. Fuck that! Instead, she stayed at a friend's

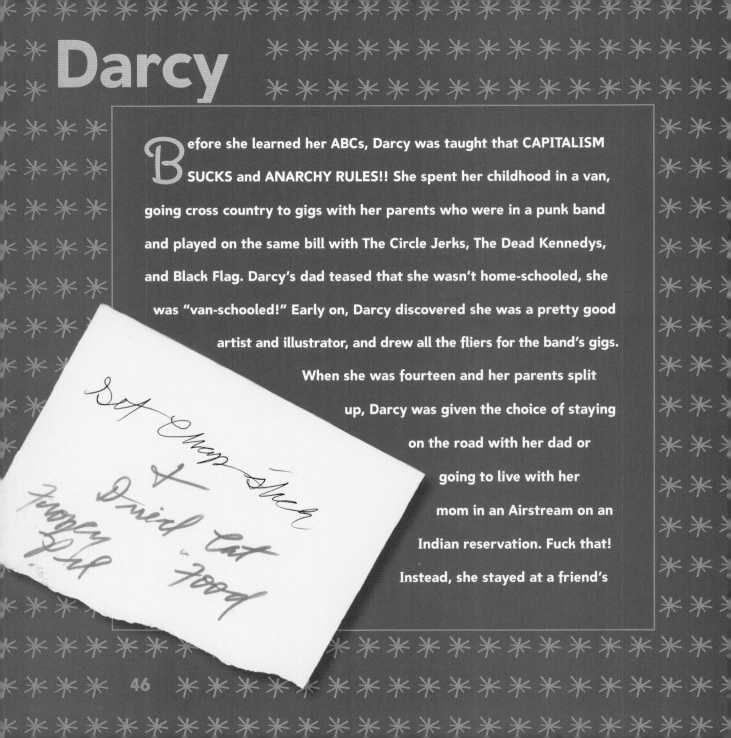

apartment and made cash any way she could—still drawing fliers for bands and working in the kitchen at a nearby nudist colony (apparently a hard position to fill so they didn't even check Darcy's age or the fake references on her "résumé"). She spent the next few years crashing on random peoples' floors till she saved enough to get a place with three roommates and her cat, Johnny Rotten. She was also able to take some time off work to focus on what she had always wanted to do—create her own comic book.

Darcy read every comic book and graphic novel she could get her hands on, and even went to Comic-Con International. The next step was figuring out what the hell her comic would be about. She knew since she felt strongly about a lot of shit (CAPITALISM SUCKS and ANARCHY RULES!!) it would have to be emo. But Darcy couldn't decide on anything beyond that. Until a few months ago, when she was up at

3 a.m., glued to a 1959 movie called *Imitation of Life*. Lana Turner plays a rising actress who takes in a black maid and her young, light-skinned daughter, and as the daughter grows older and more ashamed of her heritage, she rejects her mother by trying to pass for white.

All of a sudden it became clear. Darcy's comic would be about the ways people are ashamed of themselves, and how so many try to pass themselves off as something they're not—it's about being who we truly are, LOUDLY and PROUDLY and full of fuckin' emotion!!!

And what's the name she came up with for her comic? *Emo-tation of Life*.

# Helen

When Helen won first place in the Butler County Quilting Competition for her "Praying the Rosary" quilt, she thought her husband, Dan, would be so impressed he'd increase her spending budget. But no. Since Helen became what Dan calls "craft-crazy" in the late '80s, he's limited her weekly household allowance.

But Helen is crafty in more ways than one. She's figured out the art of coupon clipping, and saves an average of $209.00 per month on groceries! Now she can afford to buy Ka-Jinker gems for studding, Puffy Velvet

for adding dimension and texture to fabric, and more silk thread so she can finish the matching Holly Hobbie shirts she's embroidering for all her daughters and granddaughters. She knows they'll love them, even though her kids have asked her to stop making things for their families because, according to one of her sons, Joe, "Christ, Mom, our house looks like a church rummage sale!"

Dan doesn't appreciate Helen's handiwork either. He never uses the club cozies she crocheted for him when he plays golf, and when he drinks too many whiskey sours, he gets belligerent and calls her creations "Arts and Craps." But she'll show him. Her latest project is a quilt commemorating fallen soldiers from America's wars, including the War of 1812, the Civil War, World Wars I and II, Vietnam, Desert Storm, and Operation Enduring Freedom. The troops are standing at heaven's gate and Jesus is welcoming them in, arms wide open. She's been envisioning the design ever since her neighbor Betty's boy left to fight in Iraq, and knows she could win the Best in Show prize at the Smoky Mountain Quilt Show in Knoxville, Tennessee.

Just think, if she won $6,000 she could retire from coupon clipping and put *Dan* on a budget! Hallelujah!

# Kim

"I don't need no rehab or Twelve-Step," Kim often declares to her parole officer. "I can quit drinking any ol' time I want!"

With one Drunk and Disorderly and two DUIs, you'd think Kim would want to quit sooner rather than later. But besides riding her Yamaha VStar 650, drinking's about the only thing she really digs. Oh, and she doesn't mind kicking back with her old man, Casper. And riding with him. And drinking with him. They live together at the Super 8 Motel in Phoenix.

In and out of foster homes and juvenile detention centers from the time she was eight until she turned eighteen, Kim was dealt a

54

rotten hand. Once she tried to pick the top three screwed-up things in her life:

1. Never new who my daddy was
2. Ma was a f-ing junky and ended up in the slammer
3. Forsed to give up my baby

There's only one guy who can make Kim forget about the daughter she had when she was fifteen and in juvie. Jack Daniels. But just last week she got a phone call—seems the baby girl she never knew is now twenty-two, named Lauren, and wants to meet her birth mother. Kim almost wept when she heard her daughter's voice. Well, after hollering, "Whoever this really is, stop fucking with me!" and hanging up on her twice.

Kim agreed to meet Lauren, but maybe it's a mistake, she thinks: What do we talk about? What if she hates me? Should I have her over to the motel? Should I get her a present? Is she too old for a teddy bear? Should Casper be here, or just her and me? What if she looks like me? What am I sposed to say? What if she's pissed? Do I make her lunch? PB and J or baloney? What if she wants money? I ain't got two nickels to rub together. Or she's comin' to tell me she's pregnant and wants to live with me? No way in hell! Where has she been for twenty-two years? What does she want from me now? Does she know I was in juvie when they took her away from me? Does she know I just wanted a better life for her? What the fuck am I sposed to do now??

At least Kim doesn't have to figure it all out on her own. She can always turn to Jack.

# Dolores

**a**capulco, Fiji, Barcelona—these were the places Dolores dreamed of going to when she was a little girl and aspired to be a stewardess. It was a glamorous life with snappy outfits and exotic travel. She would meet a handsome pilot and they'd fly off into the sunset together.

But with her hub in Atlanta, the most exotic place Dolores has been in her fifteen years of domestic flight service has been Detroit, and every handsome pilot she's met is already married, *and* most are cheating on their wives. Ever since 9/11, with flights decreased, workers

## GET THY SHIT TOGETHER!

eggs, honey, fruit. (Apples & oranges),
Tuna, Cereal, bread for toast "~~fried~~ Raisin"
butter, brown sugar.
Muffin mix, doughnuts

laid off, and airlines declaring bankruptcy, Dolores knows she's lucky to still have a job, so she never turns down any extra shifts. If she thought she had trouble finding a man before, now with her non-stop schedule she's really challenged. Most of the guys she meets are disgruntled passengers, annoying and demanding. They're too hot, too cold, want more peanuts, need more ice, and the one request that riles her the most—when they ask for an extra pillow. If there were extras, don'tcha think they would have been offered? Passengers get belligerent, like they're taking out all their frustrations about the state of the entire airline industry—security delays, price increases, lack of food service— on her!

But then she met Bob. Frequent flier Bob Murphy lives in Cleveland and flies the 7:15 a.m. to Atlanta three times a week. It was hard not to notice the rugged, handsome businessman, especially when he opened his briefcase and took out a needlepoint he was working on! Dolores felt her hardened, cynical shell melt, and by the time they landed, Bob had cross-stitched his way into her heart.

They've been dating for a month now, when Dolores's schedule allows. But she actually didn't book any flights this weekend so Bob can come stay with her, and they can take their relationship to the next level.

Dolores is excited to have Bob sleep over. Just as long as he doesn't ask for an extra pillow.

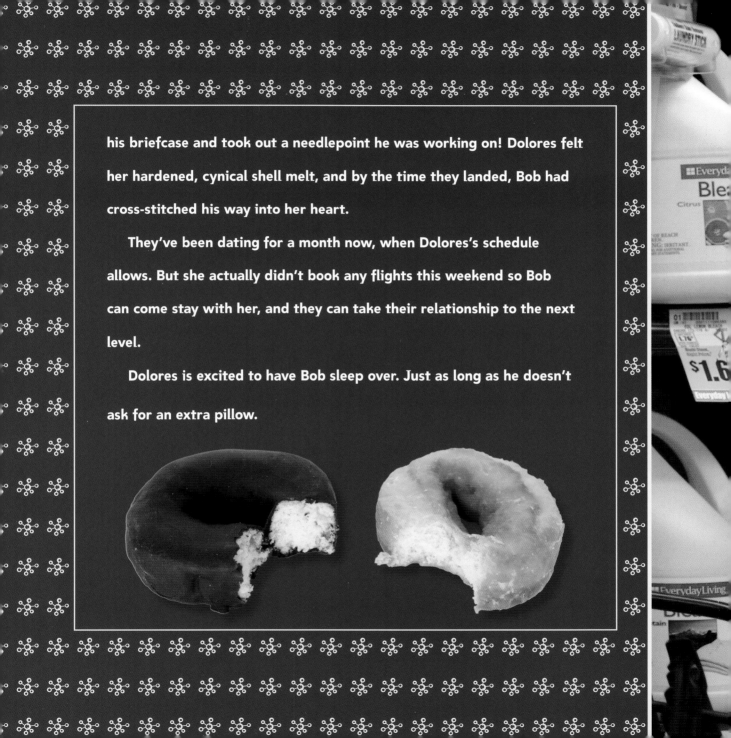

# Dr. Bloom

**G**loria Steinem is coming over for dinner. So are the head of the Feminist Majority and the president of Girls, Inc. After Dr. Bloom's last therapy patient, she'll stop to pick up a few more items for hors d'oeuvres to go with the marvelous Manchego cheese and Membrillo quince she bought at Dean and Deluca. Dr. Bloom invited the triumvirate of super-women over to elicit support for an upcoming fundraiser she's spearheading for Lifeline, a residential treatment center for at-risk teenage girls. She works closely with the organization, and even threw a Christmas party at her penthouse apartment for all thirty-six of the girls. Although jewelry was

**PROZAC®**
fluoxetine hydrochloride

1 lb. Black forrest Ham
1/2 lb. Roast Beef
1 lb. Smoked Turkey

See full prescribing information for Prozac on last pages.

stolen from her bedroom drawer, her dedication to the young women has not wavered. But, as she told her husband, Barry, a judge in United States District Court in Manhattan, "If I see one goddamn juvie wearing my mother's sapphire brooch, I'll have to be restrained."

Having worked for girls' causes ever since the *Reviving Ophelia* years—encouraging young women to be intelligent, confident, and full of self-esteem—Dr. Bloom made sure to instill those values in her two daughters. But one dropped out of school and moved in with a much older boyfriend when she was sixteen, and only calls when she needs money. The other, Bella, stopped speaking to her mother eight months ago after Dr. Bloom refused to accept Bella's third husband, saying, "You'd be better off marrying a Scientologist! At least they have career aspirations." The last words her daughter said to her were in a screaming rage before she slammed the phone down: "Nothing I do will ever be good enough for you!!" Dr. Bloom has tried to apologize several times, but how can she if Bella won't return her calls?

Of course she won't mention to Gloria or her other esteemed dinner guests that, despite being a successful therapist who has spent decades committed to empowering girls to be all they can be, her own daughters are a huge disappointment, and don't even speak to her.

# Bernadette

**B**ernadette believes that if she ran down the street naked with her hair on fire, then *maybe* someone would notice her. But that's what it would take. How could Wendy Thompson, who has been working for A-One Automotive for only two years, as opposed to Bernadette's six, be promoted above her? What's up with that?! And it's not the first time Bernadette's been overlooked at her job. It's just not fair. Bernadette works her butt off and all Wendy does is look petite, young, and white. And they all expect Bernadette to remain cheerful and not make waves—even

3 doz Hot Dog Rolls
3 doz HB Rolls.
I.C. cones
Chips
Rolls for Burger
Baked Beans.
BADERS. 4 doz.
Bananas.

Nō 00004

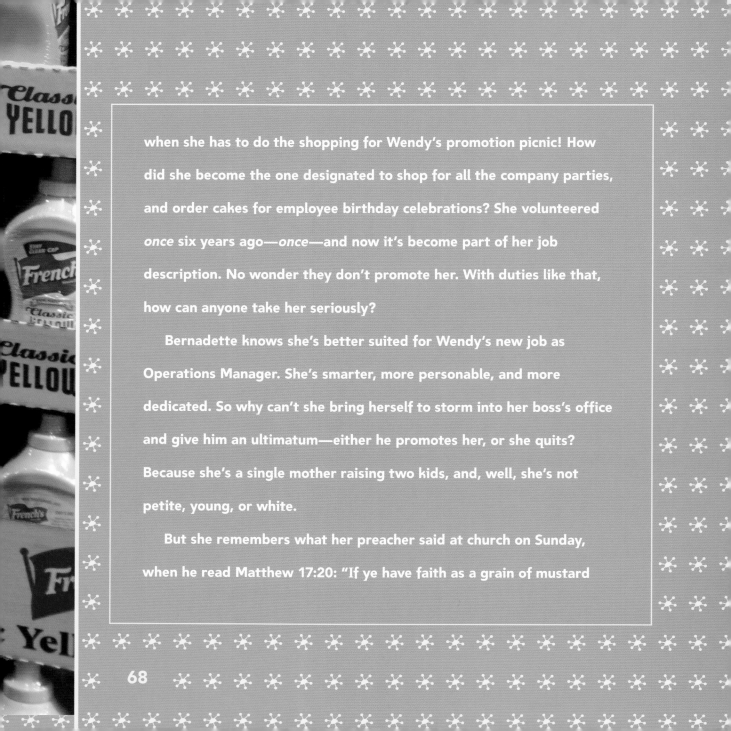

when she has to do the shopping for Wendy's promotion picnic! How did she become the one designated to shop for all the company parties, and order cakes for employee birthday celebrations? She volunteered *once* six years ago—*once*—and now it's become part of her job description. No wonder they don't promote her. With duties like that, how can anyone take her seriously?

Bernadette knows she's better suited for Wendy's new job as Operations Manager. She's smarter, more personable, and more dedicated. So why can't she bring herself to storm into her boss's office and give him an ultimatum—either he promotes her, or she quits? Because she's a single mother raising two kids, and, well, she's not petite, young, or white.

But she remembers what her preacher said at church on Sunday, when he read Matthew 17:20: "If ye have faith as a grain of mustard seed, nothing shall be impossible unto you." How, Bernadette wonders, can she have such deep faith in most things and so little faith in others— like herself?

So she's going to take the plunge. When she's done shopping and gets back to the office, she'll talk to her boss and lay it on the line. And just in case he doesn't promote her?

She'll buy some extra baked beans for her goodbye party.

# Derrick

**W**hen Derrick was five, he killed a baby squirrel by kicking it across the backyard. His adoptive mother, Marion, wondered if people were actually born cold-blooded, and started reading up on "nature vs. nurture."

Derrick's morbid bent continued through childhood as he built his own insect-collecting nets and kill jars. It seemed to Marion more scientific than destructive, how Derrick talked about the best ways for mounting the bugs that he killed—most are pinned down in the area to the right of the scutellum, grasshoppers to the right of the prothorax, and butterflies, moths, and dragonflies through the middle of the thorax—so her concern was temporarily allayed.

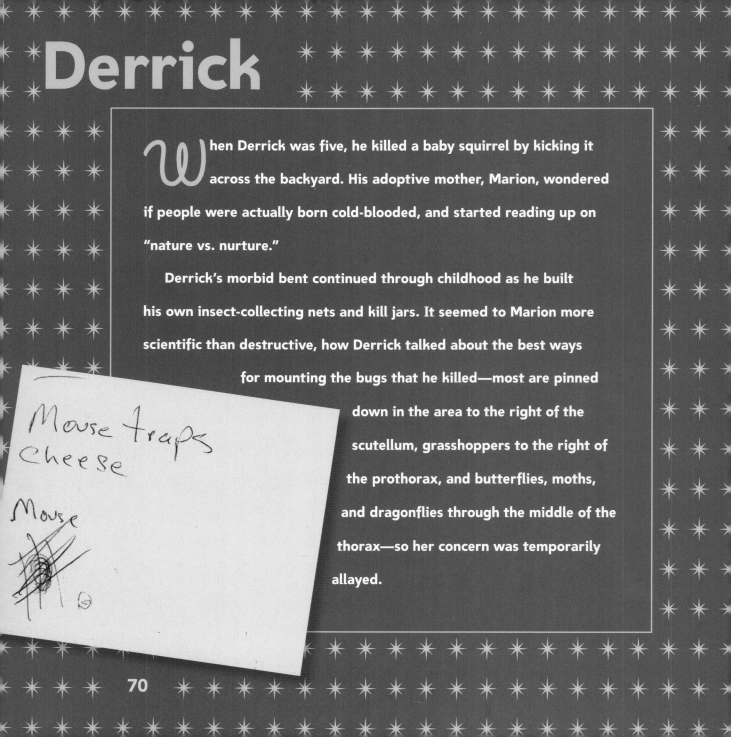

Mouse traps
cheese

Mouse

Then in his early teens, Derrick became obsessed with Ozzy Osbourne, who, he told his mother, bit the heads off of bats during live shows. Ozzy also pelted his audiences with pigs' intestines and calves' livers, and fans would bring meat and dead animals to throw back. Marion was okay with her son listening to Ozzy's music and plastering posters of his idol on his walls. But when he started researching how to build a bat house, and seeing if he could purchase a bat, she drew the line. Her other two adopted children were loving, sweet kids who played soccer and had slumber parties. What was wrong with Derrick? She finally found out when she took him to a psychiatrist, who diagnosed her son as having bipolar disorder and prescribed anti-depressants.

Despite medication, Derrick's interest in death and destruction continued on into his late teens, when he got addicted to video games and became a master at Mortal Kombat. Because he was weird, almost everyone in his high school made fun of him, especially the jocks. But Derrick managed to find a few fellow outcasts, and Marion was a bit comforted during those years. Even if Derrick was still immersed in violence, at least he wasn't killing or harming animals anymore.

Derrick's twenty-two now and Marion still lets him live at home. She thought he was doing much better—holding down a job at a shoe store and even hanging out with friends he met online. But she recently found his shopping list in his room.

Dear God, what is she to do?

# Anush

**I**F Anush's mother-in-law, Lucine, scrawls out one more of the demanding lists she's been making since she moved in with Anush and her husband eight months ago...

And **IF** Lucine makes Anush go to three different Armenian markets to make sure she gets everything she wants, just how she wants it...

And **IF** Anush's grocery-shopping skills don't live up to Lucine's standards and, God forbid, her mother-in-law bites into any large, unripe, or soft sour cherries, ranting as she spits out the offending cherries into a bowl, usually missing with her bad aim, so Anush has to pick them all up...

MKT:
A FAIRLY GOOD SIZE OF VEAL SHANKS
IF TENDER (LAMBSHANKS IF NOT VEAL
GATA IF SOFT NOT HARD.
BULK BARGAIN SOUR CHERRIES IF
SMALL RIPE AND FIRM
LAHMAJUNE IF FRESH
SPINACH BEUREG IF FROZEN
SOOJOUKA IF TEN LBS IF NOT
THEN BASTERMA

And **IF** Anush has to help squeeze Lucine's 210 pounds of flab into a girdle when company's coming, even though her mother-in-law stays wrapped in a blanket the whole time so people will feel sorry for her...

And **IF** Anush has to get down on her hands and knees to scrub the Persian rugs one more time because her mother-in-law's ancient cat urinates all over them, and then has to put up with Lucine's retort, *"You try peeing in a litter box!"*...

And **IF** Lucine orders yet another lifelike porcelain doll from the Marie Osmond Collection on QVC, then makes Anush go to the post office to send it back, exclaiming, "Lifelike? She looks dead in the eyes!"...

And **IF** the old bat spouts, "Khelket kordzadze—use your brain!" at Anush one more time...

**THEN** Anush will take the ungrateful crone to a nursing home

to show her what it would be like **IF** her son hadn't married such a

wonderful, generous, caring woman, full of restraint.

# Jet

at one time it would have seemed unthinkable that hot fashion photographer and famed lady-lothario, Jet, would settle down, but that very thing happened. Cutting loose at the Wet 'n' Wild Pool Party during the popular lesbian pilgrimage to Palm Springs, Dinah Shore Weekend, Jet met her girlfriend, Annie, when they found themselves doing Jell-O shots off of each other's breasts. Little did they know that four years later they'd be raising a child together.

Jet has tried to remain faithful, but as someone who doesn't believe in monogamy, not to mention the fact that she's surrounded by gorgeous

Paper towells
T.P.
milk
~~EGGS~~
animal cookies
pampers ! — don't forget this time !!!
Gerbers tapioca pudding
" chicken with corn
Baby wipes
apple sauce
~~diet pepsi~~
~~pancake~~ mix
commet
pick up shoes
lamp from mom's

models every day, it's been a challenge. Especially when she goes on location.

Though Annie made it clear from the start that she wanted to be a mother, Jet didn't take her seriously. She thought Annie would get over it once she saw how awesome life was with her. But last year, when Annie declared that she was getting pregnant with or without Jet, it was time for some serious self-examination. Jet had never wanted kids but did want to make Annie happy, and thought that maybe a baby would be just the thing she needed to finally settle down and stop cheating.

Nine months after getting the sperm from a friend, a hunky and closeted former model and current soap opera star, "Mark," Jet helped deliver their gorgeous baby girl, Stella. It took a while to get used to her new lifestyle, but Jet fell madly in love with Stella, and things had been going pretty smoothly. Until the debut of *The L Word*.

Jet was convinced they based the character Shane on her. And when she saw how much fun her alter-ego was having screwing around on her girlfriend, she couldn't resist diving back into the scene.

Despite her extra-curricular activities, Jet tries to be a good partner and mother. In fact, instead of going with her friends tonight to the high-profile opening of the "Labia Lounge," she's at the market, and this time, she'll remember the freakin' Pampers.

Wait...check out that hot girl by the baby wipes. As long as things are status quo at home, Annie doesn't need to know if they hook up.

Let's just hope Stella doesn't tell.

# Lloyd

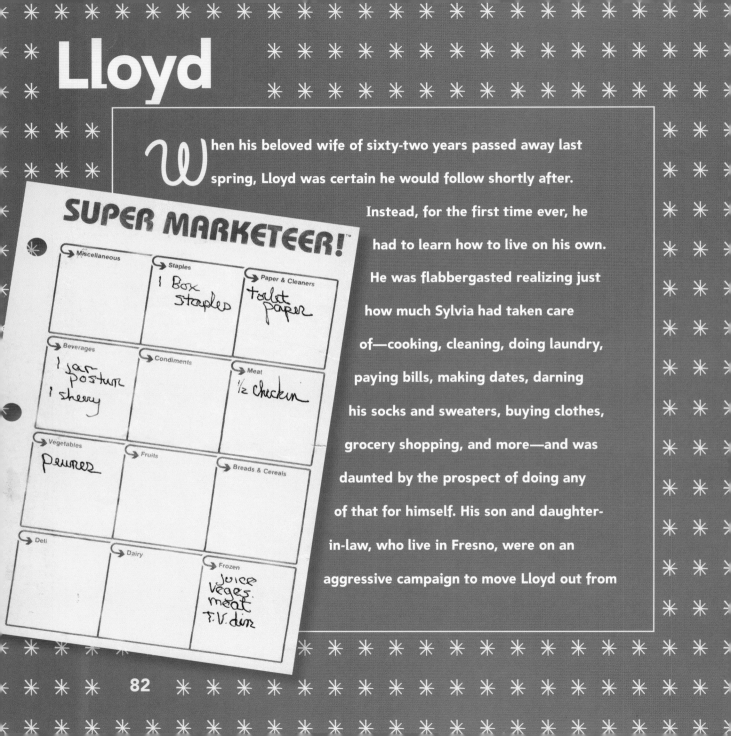

**W**hen his beloved wife of sixty-two years passed away last spring, Lloyd was certain he would follow shortly after. Instead, for the first time ever, he had to learn how to live on his own. He was flabbergasted realizing just how much Sylvia had taken care of—cooking, cleaning, doing laundry, paying bills, making dates, darning his socks and sweaters, buying clothes, grocery shopping, and more—and was daunted by the prospect of doing any of that for himself. His son and daughter-in-law, who live in Fresno, were on an aggressive campaign to move Lloyd out from

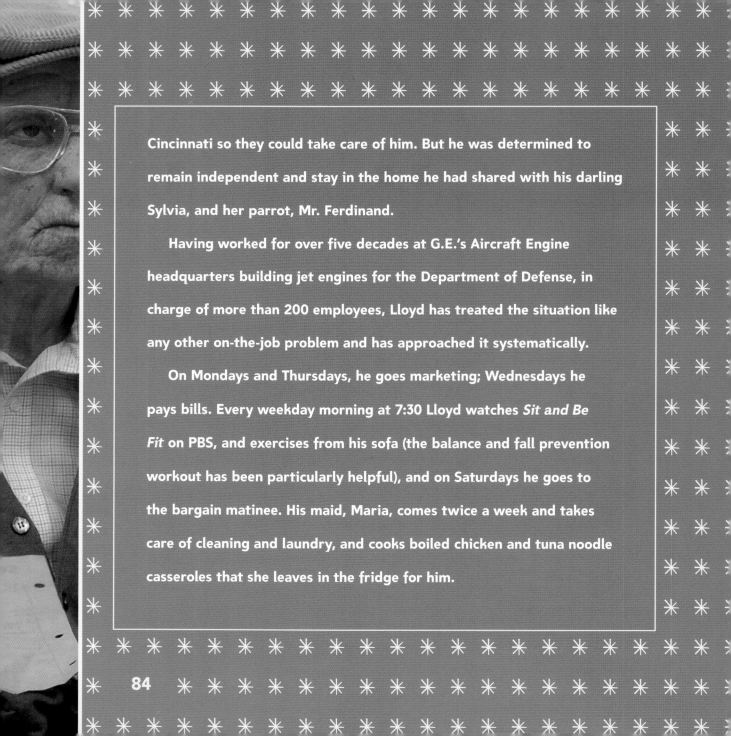

Cincinnati so they could take care of him. But he was determined to remain independent and stay in the home he had shared with his darling Sylvia, and her parrot, Mr. Ferdinand.

Having worked for over five decades at G.E.'s Aircraft Engine headquarters building jet engines for the Department of Defense, in charge of more than 200 employees, Lloyd has treated the situation like any other on-the-job problem and has approached it systematically.

On Mondays and Thursdays, he goes marketing; Wednesdays he pays bills. Every weekday morning at 7:30 Lloyd watches *Sit and Be Fit* on PBS, and exercises from his sofa (the balance and fall prevention workout has been particularly helpful), and on Saturdays he goes to the bargain matinee. His maid, Maria, comes twice a week and takes care of cleaning and laundry, and cooks boiled chicken and tuna noodle casseroles that she leaves in the fridge for him.

As isolated as Lloyd is, he's not really alone. He's still got Mr. Ferdinand, the fifty-one-year-old cockatoo that Sylvia bought when she was in her teens. Mr. Ferdinand keeps Lloyd company, spouting out phrases Sylvia taught the bird in the '50s, like "Hubba Hubba," "Wowsville, Man!" and "How's tricks, Daddy-O?" And every night when Lloyd goes to bed, it's almost as if Sylvia's still lying right there beside him when Mr. Ferdinand squawks, "Sweet dreams, Doll."

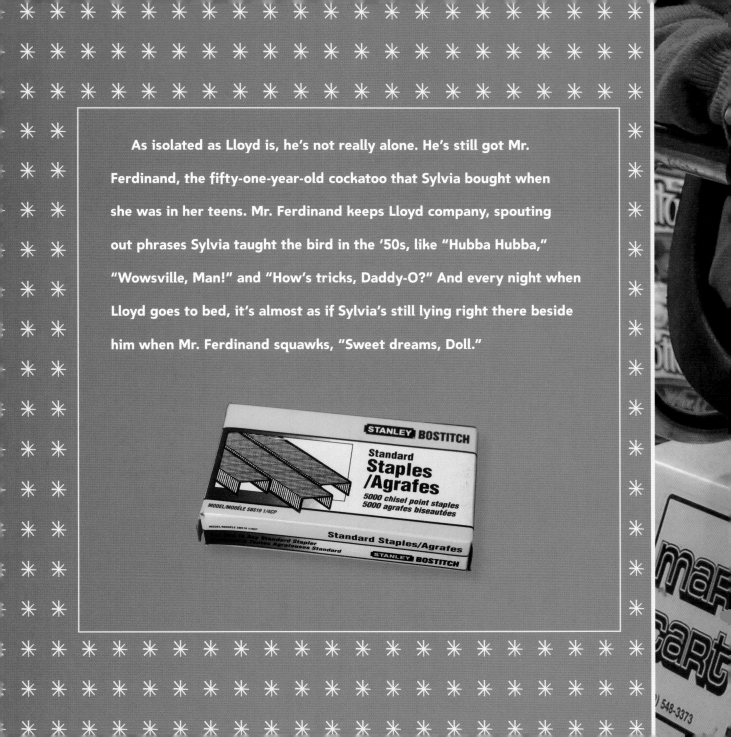

# Karen

Everyone on Karen's email list pretty much hits delete when they receive another "HELP RESCUE THIS ADORABLE DOG" flier from her. Though they respect her dedication to finding homes for abused and abandoned pets, ten to twenty emails a week is a little excessive.

Imagine how Karen feels! She has a full-time job as a veterinary assistant, running home twice a day on her breaks to take care of the fifteen dogs she rescues at a time from the pound. She's been trying to raise money so she can quit her job and focus on her mission full-time, but can never find the hours, or energy, to put

1) Pick up Geans mail & prepare bills.
2) Pick up purse
3) Pick up robe and gown
4) Take Geau Flowers
5) Clean up myself and do whatever I want.

1½) Go shopping get cat food dog n panty hose hairspray douche

together materials, a website, and everything else it would require.

Walking, feeding, brushing, cleaning up after, playing with, and finding homes for all the dogs she fosters is exhausting and feels never-ending since almost nine million dogs a year are euthanized at shelters. But who will stand up for these poor, innocent victims, saving them from their death sentences, if not Bob Barker, Doris Day, and Karen?

And now that her brother Gean has been in the hospital for three weeks with acute pancreatitis, Karen's been taking care of his day-to-day—going to his house to water his plants and pay his bills, plus bringing him things he needs to the hospital. She has no time for herself, let alone for a human relationship. Besides, none of the guys she's ever gone out with can understand Karen's devotion to dogs, and they end up leaving, anyway.

But Bill, a dogwalker she's had her eye on at the park—the one with the adorable schnoodle, Mabel—seems different. Karen's been taking a few of the rescues there every evening so she can run into Bill. And finally, after months of chit-chat, he's asked her on a date.

Karen is praying a relationship develops with Bill because if it doesn't, she's ready to send out another flier to her email list, this time for *herself* to be rescued:

"BLONDE HAIR, BROWN-EYED, BUXOM FEMALE NEEDS A LOVING HOME. Well-mannered, good disposition, she's house-trained and gets along well with men, dogs, cats, and children. Has been neglected. So appreciative of any love or attention you can give her. Completely loyal, this one's a real find."

# Troy

*I*n 2003, Troy gave up religion for Lent. Since then he's given up other things—Internet porn and swearing in front of children. But he never thought it would be so hard to kick his cigarette habit. It's been six months, and despite wearing the Nicorette patch 24/7, he craves nicotine constantly, especially when he performs in clubs. But if his new band is gonna blow up, what they need (besides a kick-ass name) is a lead singer who's in the best shape of his life. So he's cut out fat entirely, limits himself to only one beer a night (for now), and hits the gym six days a week, jock itch or no jock itch!

| Baked Goods | Baking Supplies | Beverages | Canned Goods | Condiments & Dressings | Cookies & Crackers |
|---|---|---|---|---|---|
| | Almonds | | Tomato bisque soup | Skippy Chunky PB | |
| | | | 2 can cut grn beans | | |
| | | | Vegetable broth | | |
| | | | Mandarin oranges | | |

| Cereals | Dairy | Frozen | Paper/Plastic | Pasta & Rice | Produce |
|---|---|---|---|---|---|
| | Half and Half | 1 bag mixed vegetables | Ziploc sandwich bags | Spaghetti | 5 potatoes |
| | | | Ziploc snack size | | 2 carrots |
| | | | | | onion |
| | | | | | bananas |

| Personal Care | Cleaners | Snack foods | Misc. | From Other Stores |
|---|---|---|---|---|
| Spray-on Jock itch stuff | | Blue corn tortilla chips | | |

Not smoking is also challenging at work, where Troy's a security guard at the Mutual of Omaha office building, because he mostly sits on his ass all day long doing nothing except look menacing. That's exactly why he took the job in the first place—so he could kick back and write music on his laptop during his days hanging out in the lobby, while he plays gigs at night.

So lately Troy's been making a lot of lists at work—like for his training regimen, song orders for shows, and potential names for his new band:

1. Fireballs (Alright, maybe that's just cuz of my current condition!)

2. Scattica (I like the Attica, uprising feel, but Scat sounds too shitty)

3. Smoke and Mirrors (I can just see the killer stage set for this one when we go on our world tour!)

4. Collision Course (or) Collision Coarse (or) Kollision Kourse (Hmm.

Not bad.)

   5. Let us Prey (Sounds too Christian Rock)

   6. Burn Ward (?)

   7. Dry Ice (Cool but hot. This one's awesome!)

   8. DesTroy (Hmm. It *is* my band. Do I want to use my name in the title? )

   9. Cojones (Except only Spanish speaking people will know that means "Balls." The rest might pronounce it Co-Jones. Damn, guess I really do have that on my mind right now! Why don't I just freakin' name the band Itchy Nuts?!?)

# Vera

Vera Misner is a seeker. She's tried everything from tarot to astrology, numerology to hypnosis. She jokes, "I even tried to get my palm read, but I couldn't find one gardener in Beverly Hills who would climb the damn thing!"

But Vera should have consulted her psychic before she hired Tracii, a Feng Shui expert, to rearrange the house Vera shared with Stan, her husband of thirty-four years. Three months later, the Beck Detective Agency confirmed Vera's suspicions—that her husband was schtupping the twenty-something Feng Shui-ist.

*"When the going gets tough, the tough go shopping."*™

sour cream
french bread
vermouth
vodka
sherry vinegar
avocado
lettuce (butter celery)

chili peppers
bell - pepper
×shrimp
tom. paste ✓
stew. tom.
2 lb ground chuck

1-16z can
chili sauce
salsa -
(for pasta)
sponges
frozen yogurt
cigs.

paper towels
Gelhards chili pow.
Binaca
✝samples by
Judi Krantz

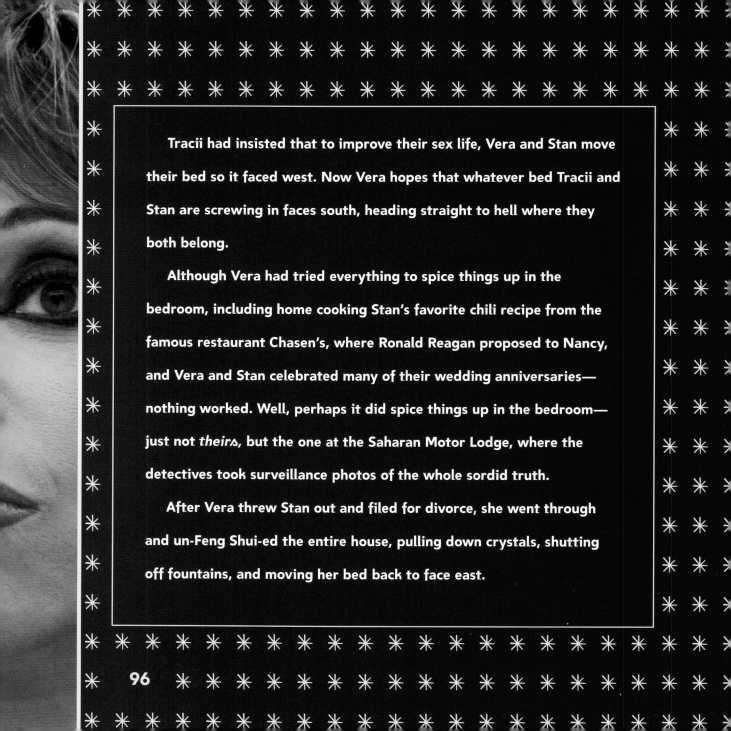

Tracii had insisted that to improve their sex life, Vera and Stan move their bed so it faced west. Now Vera hopes that whatever bed Tracii and Stan are screwing in faces south, heading straight to hell where they both belong.

Although Vera had tried everything to spice things up in the bedroom, including home cooking Stan's favorite chili recipe from the famous restaurant Chasen's, where Ronald Reagan proposed to Nancy, and Vera and Stan celebrated many of their wedding anniversaries—nothing worked. Well, perhaps it did spice things up in the bedroom—just not *theirs*, but the one at the Saharan Motor Lodge, where the detectives took surveillance photos of the whole sordid truth.

After Vera threw Stan out and filed for divorce, she went through and un-Feng Shui-ed the entire house, pulling down crystals, shutting off fountains, and moving her bed back to face east.

Although she doesn't want to spend the rest of her life alone, Vera hasn't dated in more than three decades and doesn't particularly want to remember how it's done. Especially now with men going out with younger women, she's not looking forward to ending up with some AARP-card-carrying, Viagra-popping senior citizen. *Damn that Stan!*

At a complete loss, tired of wandering around her now-empty house, most evenings Vera curls up on the couch with a dry martini and "Judi Krantz's *Scruples*."

If only her husband had some.

# Fran

"**F**ran-kenstein." That's just one of the not-so-clever names Fran's classmates called her when, between the ages of thirteen and sixteen, she had multiple back surgeries for scoliosis and even had to wear a halo, attached with metal pins in her skull. There's nothing like going from being one of the most popular girls in high school to becoming the class monster.

Fran didn't want to be a walking pity party, someone defined by high school traumas. So she got over herself when she hit twenty, and started attending Buddhist meditation retreats, went completely organic, and became a devout student of Bikram Yoga. She'd like to see any of her old classmates

*Just a note...*

Lentils,
Bread (raisin)
like carrots
Brn. Rice
nuts
peaches   apple
lettuce   potato
radish
onions
red pepper

10531NP

hold a Padangustasana pose—where you squat down in a half-lotus, one leg crossed over the other, and balance in a seated position on the toes of your other foot—for a full minute in a room that's heated to 110 degrees!

But as much as she's been working on herself, Fran still has a hard time with men. She doesn't let any get too close, and she's never really stuck around long enough to see if anyone else would. When she's with a guy, she hides under the covers or keeps the lights off so he won't have to see her scars, and rightly so—one boyfriend left after she accidentally let her guard down and he realized that she was damaged goods.

Fran recently saw the movie *Frankenstein* on TV. At first she was shaken, plunged into the memory of her adolescent taunting. But she was drawn into the scene where, after being attacked by an angry mob, the monster flees to the woods. He hears violin music coming from a shack, and the hermit who lives there invites him in. It turns out that the hermit is blind and therefore can't judge Frankenstein on his looks. He offers Frankenstein food and wine, and as the monster sits, listening to the beautiful violin music his new friend plays, he starts to cry.

Fran is just waiting for the day she will meet her own blind hermit who will love and accept her, scars and all.

# Pammy

On the '90s, when Pammy became one of the most recognized names in porn next to Jenna Jameson, she was blissfully riding the wave of success, not really thinking about the limited career span of a porn star. But when she hit thirty-five, despite her superstar status, no one wanted to hire her, and Pammy was left holding a different kind of sack.

But her porn days were not over. Determined to not only continue on in the industry that embraced her (literally), but also to revolutionize it, Pammy started Silver Foxes Productions, and has made millions of dollars shooting and directing porn films for the senior set. Using only actors above the

Coffee-mate (Hazelnut)
~~Olives~~
~~Fresca~~
~~Nair~~
Vaseline
Kleenex
~~Razors~~
Listerine Strips
~~Gummy Bears~~

Home Depot
Tarp!

age of forty, her oldest stud is seventy-five. "Pete might be shrinking in height," Pammy told *Adult Industry News*, "but definitely not in length!"

Taking the porn biz by storm, Pammy's films—including *Cockoon*, *Driving Miss Daisy Chain*, *Oldfinger*, and *Humpy Old Men*—have won numerous awards from the X-Rated Critic's Organization, and at the last Annual Adult Entertainment Awards in Vegas, Pammy was given the Golden Fist Lifetime Achievement Award.

Currently working on a motivational self-help book based on her success in porn, *When Life Gives You Melons, Make Lemonade*, Pammy has big plans to open a retirement home for aged porn stars. Using the Motion Picture and Television Fund's retirement community for actors as inspiration, the grounds will include orgy rooms specially outfitted with stainless-steel grab bars for extra support, free monthly on-site cholesterol and STD checkups, and a 250-seat, state-of-the-art theater showing Joan Crawford movie marathons and first-run porn films.

In every interview, Pammy is always asked, "Will you remain behind the scenes, or ever appear in films again?"

"It's only a matter of time," she assures her public.

In fact, she's now in pre-production on the movie that will mark her return. It's called *The Cum-Back.*

# Orlando

Of fellow Cuban Ojani Noa could work in a restaurant and end up being J. Lo's first husband, then something like that could happen to Orlando. Although, personally, he'd prefer settling down with Ricky Martin!

Growing up in Havana, Orlando dreamed of getting into show business. He fled to Miami when he was fifteen, lied about his age and citizenship, and got a job as a waiter. At age twenty-five he moved to the Big Apple, where he met Arturo, his boyfriend of six years now.

Arturo looks a lot like Ricky Martin. Well, a bald, overweight Ricky Martin. They do have the same smile and gums and, in the right light, swagger in a similar fashion.

Orlando's done everything possible to find a job in the entertainment industry. But the closest he's come

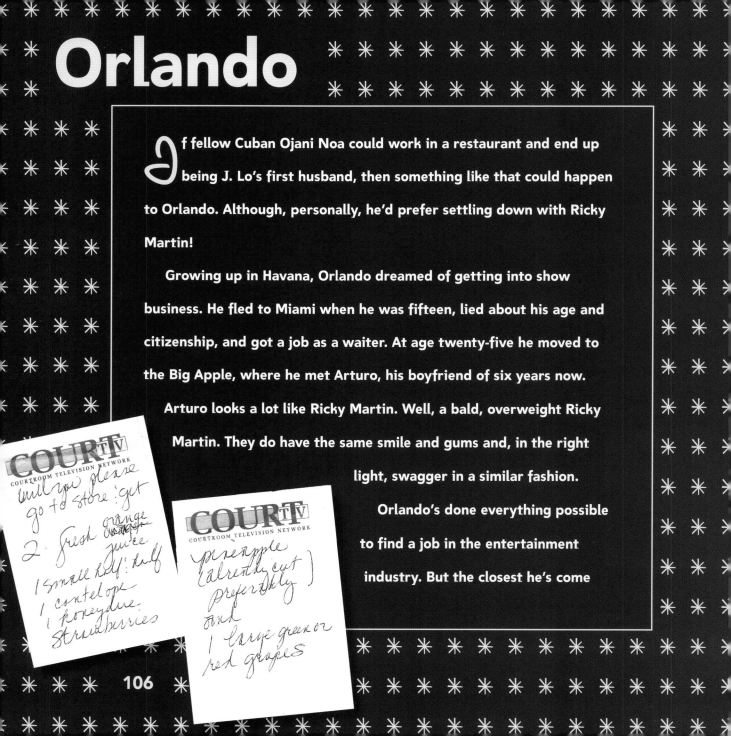

COURT **TV**
COURTROOM TELEVISION NETWORK

Will you please go to store; get
2. fresh orange juice
1 small half & half
1 cantelope
1 honeydue
strawberries

COURT **TV**
COURTROOM TELEVISION NETWORK

pineapple (already cut preferably)
and
1 large green or red grapes

106

was when he worked for a caterer and served sushi to Joaquin Phoenix at the Olsen twins' twenty-first birthday party.

Finally, after charming (rather, bullshitting) his way through an interview, he landed a job in television! He was hired to be an assistant to an executive producer at Court TV. For someone who was obsessed with watching every minute of the O.J. and the Menendez brothers' trials on the network in the '90s, the job was as exciting to Orlando as working at CBS, NBC, or ABC. He spent the week before his start date watching the channel day and night, learning about all the new shows, and coming up with some great ideas to pitch to his boss, Kelly Wright.

But all he's been doing is taking Kelly's clothes to be laundered, going grocery shopping, and running other errands for her. And, even more insulting, it turns out he was really hired to be a Manny! And not even for Kelly's child—but for her *Pekingese!* He has to cook liver for

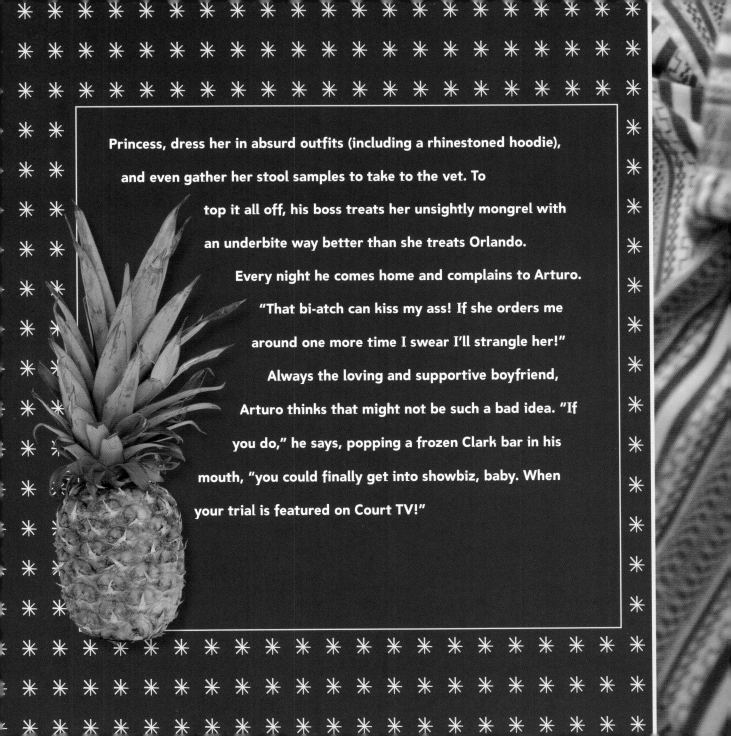

Princess, dress her in absurd outfits (including a rhinestoned hoodie), and even gather her stool samples to take to the vet. To top it all off, his boss treats her unsightly mongrel with an underbite way better than she treats Orlando. Every night he comes home and complains to Arturo. "That bi-atch can kiss my ass! If she orders me around one more time I swear I'll strangle her!" Always the loving and supportive boyfriend, Arturo thinks that might not be such a bad idea. "If you do," he says, popping a frozen Clark bar in his mouth, "you could finally get into showbiz, baby. When your trial is featured on Court TV!"

# Millie

**M**illie likes to remember. *Then* was so much better than *now*. So when Sylvia Solomon, head of Temple Emanu-El Sisterhood, asked her to share her infamous "Latke Jumble" recipe and its origins in the temple newsletter, Millie readily agreed.

Tender memories came flooding back like the rushing waters of the River Jordan:

"When I was in my twenties, so many years ago now, I was an entertainer and toured, performing in theaters throughout the country. It's actually how I met my beloved husband Myron (may he rest in peace), as we co-starred in many of these productions together.

cream of wheat
2 onions
3 Potatoes
Bread
matzah
tea Bags

The whole cast traveled on the road by bus and train, staying in motels and hotels, and although it was professional theater, we weren't making a lot of money. So we always had a hot plate. And since I was the best cook of the bunch, I often whipped up before- and after-show meals. The whole cast delighted in what they dubbed 'Millie's Famous Latke Jumble.'

Let me explain the 'Jumble' part. One night, in November 1947, we were booked to do a show in Sioux Falls, South Dakota, and let me tell you there wasn't one store that carried matzah (frankly, I don't believe I saw one Jew in the whole state either!). It was a snowy, freezing winter, and the cast was hankering for my Latkes. So I substituted bread for the matzah and, well, let's just say it wasn't kosher, but it was gobbled up clean!

Once I got my hands on some matzah in New Jersey, it was like gold and we didn't want to use it all up. So I decided from then on to use part matzah, part bread, and 'Millie's Famous Latke Jumble' was born.

I hope that, despite its break from tradition, you enjoy the recipe as much as my fellow thespians did."

Sixty-one years later, Millie can still read an audience. No need to shock the temple congregation with some of the details she left out. Like the name of the "troupe" she toured with—Lily LaRue's Burlesque Revue; the title of the show where Myron proposed to her onstage, *Then God Created Vixens*; and any mention of her show-stopping, balloon-popping finale, "Strip, Strip, Hooray!"

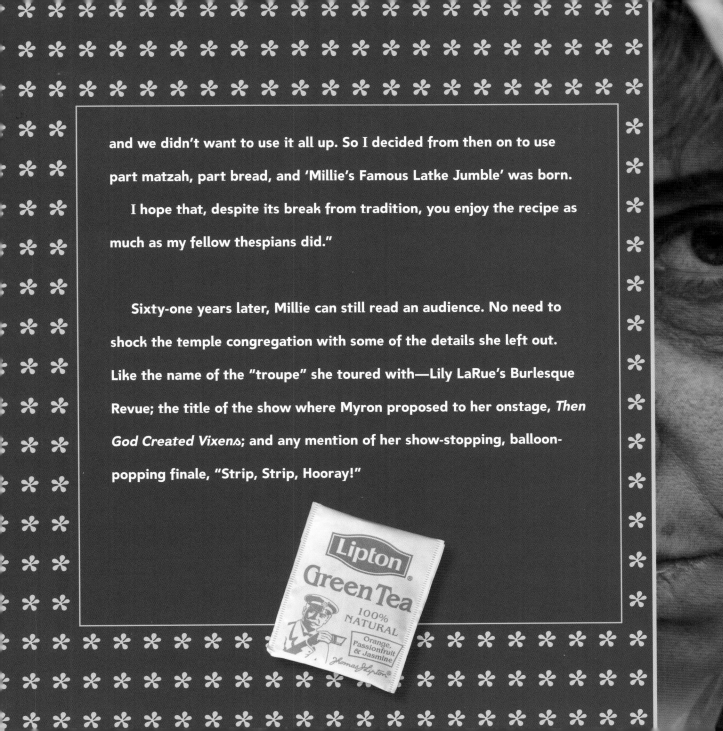

# Hillary

illary Carlip started becoming other characters when she was eight years old. One month she'd pretend to be Serena, Samantha's Go-Go boot-wearing "twin cousin" on *Bewitched*; the next month she was a sassy Carnaby Street Brit, complete with thick English accent.

Growing up, she took every left turn she possibly could, and then in 2006 she wrote a memoir called *Queen of the Oddballs: And Other True Stories From a Life Unaccording to Plan*. Her book includes tales about her escapades on the fringes of Hollywood as:

- A teenage stalker, who befriended Carly Simon and Carole King when she was fourteen years old.

- A *Gong Show*-winning juggler and fire-eater.

- A dancer in the cult classic film *Xanadu*,

- Earl Grey
- Veggies
- Papaya
- Recharge
- Cott. cheese
- Rice Dream
- Gum (Apple)

where she received valuable advice on her love life from Olivia Newton-John.

- A French cancan girl who delivered singing telegrams and was once locked in Jack Haley, Jr.'s coat closet for an hour while on the job.

- An alleged jailbird, convincing TV news and national magazines that her girl band was made up of all ex-cons.

- Several other personas she created, two of whom ended up on *Entertainment Tonight* in the same week, without anyone ever knowing they were both her.

At the end of *Queen of the Oddballs*, Hillary writes about finally coming to terms with being herself and not needing to become other people anymore.

What came next? *À La Cart*. Guess she had a relapse.

# Acknowledgments

I am so thankful to have the good fortune to continually collaborate with two wildly talented, dear friends and visionaries. The first is Barbara Green—every photograph in this book is a testament to her brilliance.

The second is Michelle Boyaner, who contributed in so many ways. Whether scouring thrift shops with me for the perfect outfit for each shopper, or helping me choose which lists to include, she always inspires me with her remarkable creativity and dedication.

THANKS A MILLION TO:

Dominie Till, whose extraordinary make-up and hair artistry helped to bring my shoppers to life, and who made the entire process completely fun and delightful. (Lifts and all!)

Chris Nelson, who I so appreciate coming out of make-up retirement to lend his mad skills in helping me become Graciela, Lloyd, Estelle, Troy, and Bernadette.

Ken Siman, publisher of Virgin Books, USA, who I can't thank enough for sharing my vision from day one, helping me find the best way to realize it, and being such an amazing, tireless partner.

Laura Lindgren, whose STUNNING book design exceeds all my expectations!

Laurie Liss, my dear friend and agent who encouraged me to stay on track no matter what others thought I should be doing.

Ann Espuelas, for doing a great job copyediting, and having such a keen eye (should that comma be there after the word copyediting?!).

Mim Eichler Rivas, who has such mind-blowing gifts, not only as a spectacular writer, but also as a *seller*, and so generously shares her gifts with me.

Allee Willis, who let us shoot PR pics at her legendary home, Willisville (location complete with shopping cart AND neon grocery store sign!).

Kristin Hahn and Charlie Stringer for their gorgeous daughter, Stella Stringer, who posed as Jet's baby.

Those who graciously gave their time to make sure my stories rang true: Vera Kessedjian, Lan Tran, Ted Lieverman, Gail Lopez-Henriquez, Thu Nguyen, Raphael Anderson-Ayers, Becky Reed, and Amy Friedman.

George McGrath, whose wigs helped me look (and smell!) like a rock star!

Everyone who has supported my habit through the years by sending me shopping lists they've found, especially William Q. Barrett.

Big Es, Saul Doll, and Goog, for being such fabulous and loving in-laws.

**LASTLY and MOSTLY:**

My mom, Mim Carlip, for being the most supportive cheerleader, and the best mother a girl could have; my dad, Bob Carlip—though he's no longer with us, he continues to inspire me every day; and my brother, Howard, for always supporting my visions no matter how out there they were/are.

My boys, Homey and Slim. All love. All the time.

Maxine Lapiduss—the everything girl. My extraordinary, generous, brilliantly talented, wholly supportive, always loving, genius partner and collaborator in every possible way. You always knew.

God, Mastermind, Higher Power, Source—whatever the name, all the same. I am so grateful, and appreciate all my blessings.